Unremitting Solace

Everything Is Within Us and Without Us

Coty Benrimoj

BALBOA.
PRESS
A DIVISION OF HAY HOUSE

Complete Jewish Bible (CJB)
Version » Complete Jewish Bible
Publisher Messianic Jewish Publishers

Testaments OT/NT
Go to: Version Information | Copyright Information | Bible-Book List
Version Information
Complete Jewish Bible
A New Translation
Dr. David Stern

Balboa Press books may be ordered through booksellers or by contacting:

Balboa Press
A Division of Hay House
1663 Liberty Drive
Bloomington, IN 47403
www.balboapress.com
1 (877) 407-4847

Printed in the United States of America.

ISBN: 978-1-4525-8991-6 (sc)
ISBN: 978-1-4525-8992-3 (e)

Library of Congress Control Number: 2014900542

Balboa Press rev. date: 02/17/2014

"Unremitting Solace" is dedicated
In memory of my loving parents
David and Raquel Abecasis
And my beloved Aunt, Bellida Abecasis

CONTENTS

INTRODUCTION

About four years ago, I came across a verse which I had never seen before and it gave me pleasure every time I read it. It made me feel warm inside and as if I already knew its meaning well. I am amazed that I had not heard of this verse before and I am including it as part of my learning through re-awakening of life's wonders and as you may well know, there are innumerable wondrous blessings. It is from 1 Corinthians 13:4-8 and two of my dear friends have its contents for beautiful view on one of their walls. My two other dear friends who recently renewed their wedding vows after 50 lovely years of marriage, also had this verse read aloud during their ceremony. I am happy to have come across this wonderful saying twice in the last several years:

LOVE

Love is patient and kind, not
jealous, not boastful,
not proud, rude or selfish, not easily angered,
and it keeps no record of wrongs.
Love does not gloat over other people's sins
but takes its delight in the truth.
Love always bears up, always trusts,
always hopes, always endures.
Love never ends; but prophecies will pass,
tongues will cease, knowledge will pass.

1 Corinthians 13:4-8

Many years ago I recognized that I had the strong desire to write a book. I wasn't sure what I wanted to express in it but strange as it seems, it was a strong yearning which I had developed. As life evolved I retained this desire in the back of my mind, always there, never parting but I hadn't the vision of what it would contain.

In the summer of 2011 I woke up at 4 a.m. and grabbed a composition book and started writing automatically. I didn't stop in the course of one hour. This is how this book emerged, mostly written in the wee hours of the morning and automatically, transmersed in a dream and not knowing what I was about to write and forgetting what I had written.

Two and a half years later my book took form and it came to me how to organize it. Something that also occurred in the course of the last three or four months was the writing of the poems. I once wrote a poem and only one in my entire life. Last summer I unexpectedly started writing poems automatically as again, I inadvertently had the impulse to do so. This is what transpired and I wrote 52 poems in the course of the summer.

I am in amazement, since I don't plan writing at any time but it happens at a given time as if it's pouring out of my soul. Once it happened while I was showering and another time while I was driving and I had to stop at the side of the road where six new poems were born, two of which were written in Spanish, my first language. For the most part, I wake up in the early morning and start writing poems as well as context.

I conclude by sharing that before I decided to write this book, my dream was to become a motivational speaker. It may well be why I joined Hospitality Toastmasters of La Mesa, California in 1996. I worked on my first manual and achieved Competent Toastmaster. In 2009 I joined Palomar Airport Toastmasters, Carlsbad, California, and worked on two manuals and achieved Advanced Communicator Bronze. At the moment I am a member at Holistic Business Toastmasters, Encinitas, California and working on two manuals to achieve Advanced Communicator Silver. My dream is to become a motivational speaker and toward enhancing my speaking abilities for this purpose. I believe that I'm on my way to becoming that which I've yearned for such a long period of time and like the writing of this book, it may well happen un-expectantly one of these days! I now understand the purpose behind this book. To enable, empower and support, to nourish, to instill love, patience and understanding and send love and maintain it myself through sharing my knowledge and experience in life. In navigating life, my purpose, it seems, has been to be a source of love and kindness to whomever I encounter. I know that I will never be perfect but I know I will not stop trying.

This book has been sent to me by a higher source and I am feeling the necessity to write my thoughts and offer it to those who wish to absorb it. In the end, isn't this what life is all about? Using our own true free-will?

ACKNOWLEDGEMENTS

Special thanks and acknowledgement to Patricia Ariadne, Ingrid Arnold, Kanita Bari, Jacob Benrimoj, Leah Ruth Benrimoj, Mark Eleazar Benrimoj, Violeta Alegria Abecasis Beach, Gaga Barnes, Khevin Barnes, Stephanie Casey, Arianna Choza, Paul Choza, Maggie Ann Clark, Ribca Abecasis Delarosa, Gentila Norah Abecasis Espinosa, Miriam Guberek, Hannah Hall, Ann Heppler, Geetha Krishnan, Madhu Kurbetti, Siddharth Pujari, Linda Levier, Grace G. Madsen, Richard A. Madsen, J. Adam Milgram, Sandy Milgram, Marilyn Peterson, Sarah (Ena) Pinto, Ruth Platner, and Barbara Tanksley, whom without their love, guidance, acceptance and friendship my heart would not have grown to the space it is right now and therefore I am so grateful for their support and loving presence in my life which has made a difference in the writing of my first book, "Unremitting Solace."

QUOTES BY COTY ABECASIS BENRIMOJ

1. "See and you shall find a mirror of yours and mine."
2. "Yesterday is a memory, tomorrow is a dream and today is a moment in bliss for me."
3. "Live the life you want to lead as yours and no-one else's."
4. "Transforming one-self by changing our thoughts is indicative of changing our life's course."
5. "Be sincere with yourself and you will regret nothing."
6. "Behave in a way in which you would want to be treated and love what and how you live."
7. "Know that we make big and small errors and start pardoning yourself as well as others."
8. "Be happy, be healthy and stop blaming others for your own predicaments."
9. "Treat yourself often to that which makes you happy."
10. "Smile a lot and shine on."
11. "Cry and don't regret it – cleansing is good for the soul and soul living."

12. "Save yourself every day of worrisome thoughts and deny them inflicting upon you."
13. "Tame yourself slowly and lovingly because we can."
14. "Induce laughter, reduce stress and live more contented and peaceful."
15. "Laugh all the way to new health with Laughter Yoga."
16. "Seek laughter and you will find serenity, find serenity and you will live in love of laughter."
17. "Laughter makes people of all cultures feel connected, meet and bond."
18. "Enjoy laughing for no reason, NO BOOZE, just intoxicating laughter."

CHAPTER 1

PEACE

Who are we? It's not about how we look in the exterior; it's how we feel internally. We've got to learn how to feel, feel our emotions, analyze our emotions and deal with our emotions. Accept who we are as true human beings. Use what you got – and you've "got a lot". Feeling is the most important part of life. If you're not the most becoming individual in the earth, that's ok, we aren't able to change our looks too much, but if you feel great, exude contentment, believe in yourself and stop making *COMPARISONS, YOU WILL LEAD A MORE PEACEFUL AND CONTENTED LIFE*. It is within you and it's also without you, you choose, use what you got, don't let life pass you by unknowingly and become entertained with the illusion that we are all here and should be this way or that way – NO – <u>We are, I am.</u> We are beings and intrinsically support our higher selves if we so believe to serve a higher purpose. One way to lead and serve a beautiful and contented life is to become so involved in being, that there's no wasted time in competing with others, comparing ourselves with others, or maintaining a "certain" perception of how people view us. We are FREEEEE beings – we are – we just are!

Behave in a way you wish to behave, bearing in mind your true self is reflected in everything you do. Be aware, aware of yourself, the space around you, and the people surrounding your circle. Acknowledge these – know that you are where you are supposed to be. Do not fear – because there *IS NO FEAR. THERE JUST ISN'T!* Perform your life in a "moment" attitude. Know yourself. Know that you are "great" just the way you are. Knowing this, you may choose to transcend and become different, better, more courageous, fearless, knowledgeable, in praise of people, motivator of all and all whom pass your way; doing this at no cost, just to be you, who you truly are, a wonderful, wonderful being; a responsible, loving and caring being.

Again, do not fear, for fear is just an illusion of the mind. It's there to confuse and berate us at times! Do not let that Be: Be who you are, know who you are; Be the person you are; never judging nor condescending, critical but only loving, compassionate and absolutely in love with love and life. Lead the life you are supposed to lead, calm, tranquil, in love with the whole world and the whole of creation inclusive of your perceived enemies and friends. Know All. Know what you are about. Do this well. Acclaim faith and release doubt, acclaim love and release hatred, acclaim responsibility and release lethargy, acclaim perfection and release imperfection, release imperfection and acclaim love; love for all humankind.

Imagine everyone in this vast and beautiful Universe being in love of each other, floating about daily in floods of pure crystalline waters. Waters which run clear of mud and residue, delighting ourselves in warmth; warmth of being and loving, expecting nothing, wanting nothing, living because we are. We are in contentment of the soul being, intrinsically just being. Forget what you learned in this material realm, forget and begin to remember, remember the Self. The self is unconditional love. Love which is pure and forgiving; love is a beautiful feeling.

Why do we always want to be loved? Why do we lead our lives wanting and needing to be loved? We've heard all about it – like in the news! "Hear All About It", "Hear All About It". We strive to receive love but what we don't realize is that love is what we need and we *need* to give it to be able to receive it. That's as simple as asking for food. If you want and certainly need food for survival, we have to go and get it – if we don't get it we don't survive! – Love – If we don't give Love – we don't get it, it's as simple as that. Try it! In understanding this concept, we may understand much of life's simple treasures that is within our reach.

Some people don't want to risk giving love because of their fear of being hurt, their ego is great and when love may not be reciprocated then we just shut off. NO, do not shut off, be strong, and feel higher than a towering mountain, never withering, tall and complacent to all types of climates. Be receptive to all that is given, including love, even if it's is not received or accepted. Our duty is not to care why it's not accepted, our duty is to give, give, give, give. Give *Love* no matter if it's accepted or not, I repeat. I don't mean sex; sex and love are not the same. Love can come in many different forms and if we don't recognize it, we may lose it when it arrives as a hidden blessing. Love thy neighbor; love is what I'm talking about. "Just Give It"; just give it up, give love to everyone in your path! Don't expect anything back. "*LOVE IS ENDLESS POTENTIAL*." Do not worry for "this is it". When you are able to love everything and everyone – *AND THAT'S A WHOLE LOT*"! You are able to "Be" and when you are able to "Be," you are then able to resist temptation, understand what it is and enjoy a life with wealth irrespective of financial stability. Enjoying the gratitude that is in our heart; enjoying life as it is and it always was – with infinite FAITH, tranquility and in introspection, learning the *IMPORTANCE* of reaching for the true meaning of "who we really are?" Asking ourselves, "*Who Am I?*" "*Why Am I here?*"

SOLACE

When in doubt seek solace
In our souls lies it
Be in touch with splendor
Splendor becomes wonder
Wonder becomes comfort
And comfort soothes and consoles
In the end it so heals

INSPIRE LOVE

Self-acceptance is beauty
Going Within brings joy and peace
Small pleasures like smiles
Bring happiness
Loving ourselves unconditionally first
All Joy remains within

Chapter 2

RESILIENCE

How many of you have had confrontations with people – why not? No! I'll share through some way of comparison of how we may keep these unpleasant memories stored in our minds serving us uselessly. How many of you are familiar with computers and storage of files? The same as with filing systems, computers have places or libraries where we can store our files. We can save our files or may it be our "memories" in a filing folder in a place, desktop or other. The mind also has this capability. We decide what is important to us and store the memories in an easy and accessible place such as the desktop if we're talking about ease of access because we open up the computer - there it is – right in front of us on the desktop!

We may store our memories much in the same way and where-ever it pleases us. For example: occasionally our memories are great and full of wonderful feelings and emotions and if we decide within ourselves that we wish to access this place of beauty and being with contentment, we then, automatically, when the innate decision has been formed, we store it in an accessible place if we want to truly be happy and use it to lubricate our feelings and engulf ourselves in happiness.

On the other hand if we decide that we don't want to retain happiness, and believe me, "we do", then this memory of grief, sadness or feelings of fear and so forth become stored in an easy accessible place for us to access when we want to validate this attention of victimization, in order to self-allude and more. Therefore, "we are what we think." The challenge is that we are living habitually and wandering about life feeling like a zombie, not realizing that we are able to "choose." In choosing for our well-being, we would then store happy memories in our so called "Desktop" to retrieve and allow ourselves happy thoughts of whichever content makes us happy. We allow life's flow but we do this because we have decided to live fully and it could or could not be a conscious choice. We all have it. We have the ability to know what is good for us but sometimes for unknown reasons, the unconscious maybe, does the opposite of that which makes us happy and we become the victim, the persecutor or even the rescuer and keep these thoughts or memories if you will, looping around in these compartments!

Until we realize –*and this could happen in this lifetime for us, or not!* And until we allow ourselves the total acquisition to joy, love, faith and all which is good for our souls, until then, and only then – we have arrived. Arrived to the understanding and the power of being who you are in essence, a pure and unwavering source of light which can shine through you and beyond you just the same as you can amp up an electronic device – it's up to us and only us.

Start today, by amplifying your energy circuit and conduits. Make a pledge to yourself by choosing a path of unconditional love for yourself, a constant opportunity of realized responsibility to yourself and start taking care of your innate soul who can guide you to peace, happiness and prosperity by igniting it with warm and recognizant thoughts for yourself and consequently for others.

We are in control and only us. We can navigate the Web or not, we can drive ourselves to happiness or to sorrow. We choose. Choose the good way I suggest; be content and happy with fulfillment of your dreams! We do not need to hear voices outside of ourselves any more. What we need for our own well-being is that: "Well" – "Being". Be well and acknowledge the importance and clear necessity of what your soul wants and needs and you'll be directed inwardly for the better, whatever your known or unknown purpose in life is. Be kind to yourself – accept yourself as you are *now*! Accept the love that you are and encompass it; if you will. Do not be indoctrinated by others' wills – use "your own good will." Be mindful of the overactive mind because the mind will endeavor confusion. Stay firm in your convictions. Know within yourself what's right or wrong for you, and go with it. Listen to it – that is - your inner will. You'll know what you need because then when you are more aware, this awareness will direct you and you'll learn how to listen to your heart and soul at times when the yearning is there and you'll know. You'll also know when to employ your mind for mundane things of life, like using it enormously well when working and making a living, when making decisions in life that need to be made and go forward.

When you are in love with yourself – and I don't mean in love with your selfishness, your own body, narcissism; I mean when you are cleansed and live with your own understanding of unconditional love, you know when to switch to mind and mindfulness and when to switch to work-gear as I say. Same as when we are working on the computer, we are constantly changing, creating, navigating, suddenly we change gears, we may for example, decide to stop and drink or eat, or we may want to continue working on it. We can also switch from being to doing and from doing and being and keep balanced as needed.

We are a vast knowing intricate human machine as I describe it at times. Intricate we are. As we know, our bodies and minds are amazing. Endlessly learning with love and responsibility for oneself and continue developing on a conscious level. At times, we may also develop unconsciously, in whichever way it manifests itself is fine, just as long as you persevere and listen to your intuition. There is nothing wrong in desiring for ourselves. A desire to open a business, or to travel the world, to make your life healthier, anything is possible. I'm not saying it's going to be easy. Remember when some of us had to learn a new language because of college majors, requisites etc.? Or we had to take a job that wasn't interesting to us because we had to for reasons beyond our control or anything we've had to put up with. At times we just have to do things and they are not easy. By doing things we are not endeared to, we bring more development and more sense of being and more power to our lives. We become who we were not. If we were impatient, we become more patient, if we were bored we develop new skills.

Our story goes on because after all, life is all about stories. And stories that we want to tell, stories that we don't want to tell and stories that we tell ourselves. At times our stories are unreal as we may choose to lie to ourselves as well as to others. We may want to escape reality and that is a good way of becoming depressed. We keep stories and all it is, is life that has happened to us. We don't need any of it if it is to boast about ourselves, feel more connected to others, gain sympathy, empathy, or even acquire notoriety. If we use our stories in such a way it isn't doing us any good. Rather, go on without this type of behavior. Stories which express selflessness, and the object of telling it is to support and encourage others or employed in giving loving messages and so forth, those stories bring joy and completion and may preserve others besides ourselves as well. Being kind to ourselves is the secret of life because life begins with us and only us. In finding a way, we strengthen our resolve by becoming aware of what we are facing.

EMPATHY

Compassion is here to stay
When we are graced with a mainstay
Of self-reliance and abreast
Of wonders pronounced
Surrounded by and bound
By truthful alliance
To this heritage of ours

RESOLVE

Gazing, yearning, building strength
Strange encounters stride through
Begging, wanton, undecided
Bellowing in the winds of no return
Year, yearn, yearn
For outward yet inward luminescence

WITHOUT AND WITHIN

Besides temptation do we know?
Learning through our mistakes should be our joy?
Why then blind ourselves more?
Showing the strength we don't own?
Uphold yourself with all your might
And do not cause yourself any more fright
It's what we need to exercise
In a way that is longstanding
Remain rebirthed, redeemed, rebound
And live the life you so earnestly have found
In the origins of all that is sound

Chapter 3

ALIGN

When we take care of our minds our bodies will follow. We all know how anything works, be it a car, computer or any device. A brain makes the functions work. If the brain becomes rusty, it cannot function at top capacity and starts lagging. Being able to recognize this in terms of our aliveness and awareness, all of what's needed to retain full capacity and go full motors ahead is to continue learning, doing (and also being), advancing in our development making our own lives easier to flow and merge. Already knowing that we cannot make others' brains or engines work, we can only polish our own capacities and our faculties with that which makes us whole. We cannot make it for anyone else but for ourselves! Becoming who we are right now, accepting who we are right now and loving who we are at this moment and always.

Without overly thinking, the mind has a break. What happens when we have breaks? When we take a break we relinquish ourselves to relax and renew and we may then continue our life's quest and we align ourselves with the Universe. Taking breaks may include a myriad of things such as exercise, meditation, reading, hiking or any activity which takes you beyond. When I say beyond, it means beyond the doing, "I" thinking analogy. For example, when I'm swimming in the ocean, which is one of my favorite summer pastimes, I am relaxing in the moment. For me, although I'm exercising and moving, I'm in exquisite ecstasy because I'm totally engulfed in the moment. The waters caress me and make me go to a place that is a wonderful place for me. It's like a whole new dimension of space. For me, being submerged in the sea is all that I need for that moment to bring healing to all my body. Although my initial intention is not for this healing but because I enjoy it so much, it does just that. It heals me because I am enjoying myself utterly and immensely which the senses interpret as "wow" moments and good feelings are what nurture the soul.

Whether or not feelings are good or bad, nevertheless, they are "your" feelings. As I described earlier, we can bring about desires of feeling good or we can bring desires of things that bring us misery. We are in control. When we bring happiness to our souls, it's the same as replacing or refilling the oil in the tank of your car – without *refilling and taking care of that which needs some type of infusion, it decays and becomes rusty and then fails to work at our highest potential or maybe not at all*. When one part of the engine fails, the connecting parts also may become contaminated and we all know how that is. Talking about cars and engines, one thing leads to another and before we know it, we need to dispose of the car as it no longer can carry us wherever we need to journey to. Same would happen to our bodies – wouldn't you know? If we keep degenerating, maybe first with, say, our gums get infected; we lose health there, sometimes the unhealthy gums can manifest heart trouble. In any case, we would maybe also end up losing our teeth; this brings new issues one would need to cope with. For example, not only you have zero teeth, you now need a dentist to make a denture or implants. This will be an added expense and time consuming. If we had been more responsible to take care of our gums at the first sign of their deterioration, all this time and cost would have been eradicated and we would have had time for pleasurable things. I'm not saying that we need to enjoy life to the extent that we are going to let go of things that need to be addressed. "Always do your best in taking responsibility for your health." My intention is not to undermine the individuals who may have had this type of circumstances happen to them.

Although these types of circumstances may happen to all of us, we do not need to blame ourselves forever for our misgivings. We need to "grow up" and face ourselves, as I've mentioned earlier. We need to look at ourselves and not our neighbor. It is easy to look at other people's flaws and not ours. Have you ever heard someone recount a story about their friend, where when you really look at it, it's not their friend, it's their own story and they do not want you to know it's them? Come on, be real, say it, it's "you" deal with it, "ask for support", you will get it. Ask, ask, ask! Ask and you shall receive, isn't that the quote? Same analogy can be used in all types of different scenarios, whether it's ignoring signs of beginning of diabetes disease, which is the largest growing health issue in America, or eye problems, digestion, you name it. We need to be aware of how we feel and what our brains are telling us and cues as to how we are feeling. Are we feeling sad, happy, angry or frustrated? We need to recognize our impending feelings and become more and more responsible in resolving daily issues that arise. Don't brush it under the carpet, this is so easy to do, and I have done this. I believe we all do it. We negate, deny, accuse others for our problems, delude ourselves and so forth, but when it comes down to it, we are the ones in control just as the car that has degenerated. The only difference is that the car needs someone to pour oil in the oil tank etc. as for ourselves; we cannot rely on someone else to do our "soul work". We need to lubricate our wheels, our souls, and our minds serving ourselves to do this by means of anything we think can support our well-being, be it by meditating or a large variety of available ways of maintaining ourselves healthier. We can find support from friends, spouses and relatives as well as professional support when the journey gets tough. "When the going gets tough, the tough get going" this is a good expression. Ultimately the ball is in "our" court and only we are the receiver to initiate and create harmony in our lives to own an exulted state of being. Reach for that ball, grasp it with all your might – it is yours to do what you please with it. Throw it far or throw it near but throw it, you decide, you are in control and "you can do it!" And "do it" you will. Become a source of continued resilience, whatever age you are. Become whole by accepting who you are, a light and shining bright. Believe in yourself. Bathe yourself with a river of love towards yourself unconditionally, and you shall be whole again.

SUCCEED

Moving water, rivers do
Like the moon lovers realm do prosper
Letting, living, dooming done
End the heavy current's wrath
Live renewed, rebirthed, redeemed
Something we intend pursue
When the canals do cleanse
Doing with or without
Live well, accept, receive

GROWING PAINS

Shadows, darkness, fears, delusions
Dwelling in caves of fogginess
Unsure, redundant at will
Seeking collective acknowledgment
Unready of unveiling circumstance
Expecting, relying and unrelenting
Become aware of these
And set yourself free

THE UNIVERSE

The Universe is working in true perfection
Supporting and guiding us to unison
In health, prosperity and in love of thyself
Of all there is to have and to hold
Eradicate abuse and store no hate
For we are innately held
In fortitude and thirst for what we uphold
To be the best for the future to hold
Remain to live a worthy truth
Believing your strength is innately yours
And add it to your resume of wills, will you?

CHAPTER 4

INTELLECT

Once upon a time I was victim to my own thoughts and maybe you might relate to this somewhat. I've heard of people confiding in me about the "mind chatter." I myself have observed this and recognize what they are talking about. Many years ago I was getting bombarded by a large proportion of thoughts which were not very uplifting at all, on the contrary, they were fearful and worrisome. I then decided I would not listen to these thoughts any longer and started to ignore and dismiss them from my mind. I then made a great habit of continually doing this and it took years to become an expert at this practice but it has worked for me. It worked so well that I became owner of my own thoughts and had non-turbulence in my own life, internally, that is. I was at peace because I was denying my mind to run away with itself and keep me chained to feelings of unworthiness, fearfulness as well as worries. I became my own master and minded what I wanted to mind and I did not listen to the mind chatter and my disparaging thoughts of disdain and un-restfulness. I did not tell of this to any soul as I was working toward my own health and one cannot be a preacher, as I have found people don't want to listen and when they sometimes do, they fake it and often times end up changing the subject. Therefore, I continued my sole journey in working for myself and make things better for myself as I figured that if I felt innately great, I would be able to pass on any contentment to others.

Don't think for one moment that I wasn't majorly disturbed at times, no! I was in turmoil many times but it was not a constant battle. It was when circumstances beyond my control made me feel helpless and then of course I wasn't at peace because I hadn't learned to surrender to what is, at that time. I hadn't quite understood this frame of mind, the feeling of surrender and comfort in my being. When I understood to surrender to a higher power, I then felt peacefulness more because it made me stay positive as I innately am. Not that everything will become a bed of roses but if I can help it, I'll make it one for myself and my inner peace.

After a lifetime of experiences I have realized, maybe pretty late in life for solace, but surely very happy to be here and now in this space of mine. A space we can all create or re-create, if you will. We are the only ones that are in control of our being. Ourselves with our mind, our intellect, our emotions, our desires and most importantly, our love towards ourselves and others can and make the world a better place one moment at a time. We belong to this beautiful Universe full of exquisite opportunities of faith and we can give so much in the way of words.

We can also give in the way of silence as well, as you may remember that "silence is golden." Think when there is no need to voice anything at all, even if we do not agree with what we're experiencing, we can and are able to keep centered and feel the goodness that we have and not have to converse or give our opinions because we can listen and be silent and all is well. When we start looking at differences in other people's way of living we engage in something that is totally unnecessary to voice, in my way of thinking. We all are living to learn or not to learn our own lessons, because after all, these lessons are present to teach us something. In meddling with differences and becoming competitive or jealous all we do is bring up dissatisfaction. When we become dissatisfied with others, I suggest in retroceding and giving up tolerating their ways if it's going to affect us. If in turn, their differences do not affect you, it certainly is a sign that we have become centered and in this grounding we are at peace and can continue on well with no outside aggravation. Everything is within us and without us when I remember this state of mind.

Our intellect of course serves us well and we can use it for great purposes. Things that appear to be a tad discomforting and painful could be a great opportunity for succeeding in becoming more tolerant and tolerance brings peace and acceptance. Then peace and acceptance brings faith in ourselves to stay positive in mastering the mind-self which in turn brings knowledge, wisdom and power, and power to bring about positive changes in our lives. Before we totally listen to someone's suggestion to a better way of living for you, I believe that we cannot blindly accept what is being propositioned. Everyone has lived a completely different life to yours so what would work for them may not work for you.

Remember to keep being kind to yourself, same as the saying "charity begins at home." We need to start with ourselves – "it starts here, inside of us." No-one will ever completely understand where you are coming from even if it seems to them it's clear in their mind because they have not walked in your shoes. Be real and accept your own fortune and be grateful of all the attributes you were endowed with from the start because all of us are born with a tremendous amount of these for us to possess and use. Use them in love and in kindness. When we use what we got and I repeat, "We got a lot," we are giving of ourselves and it is said that giving is the best feeling. This being said, we also need to learn to receive.

For me, receiving has been a bit of a challenge, not sure why, yet as my journey continues, I reach to learn more and use what I learn for my own benefit as well as for the benefit of others. In fine-tuning our amazing fortitude, we realize what a great source of blessing we are and what a great person we all are. Believe it and feel it and go on and reassure yourself a quintillion times of this and never despair because intellect joined with love and wisdom becomes a tremendous source of power for us which we can use daily and lead a blissful, remunerative and a life-scene which is surely to endear us to everyone in this Universe for years to come.

LISTEN

Be like waves which crash on the jetty
Washing all our impurities away
Waves like a crescent curtain
dangling in its fringes
Unearthing sunken precious stones
Hurling them up above the elevation
Hanging on dear life right ahead
Waves that don't crush us because we wish it
Waves that surface and in turn are subdued
Waves we are in this depth of consciousness
Appeal to and unearth your Godly wisdom
Uphold and hang in the untimely crush
Be strong, be heard, be known and be well
For all will suffice at the end of the spray

RETURNING

Unfamiliar faces torn and wretched
Reflecting on wanton, unaffected
Cry in the darkness, cry and get in touch
For all that's bursting from the crust
Crust in the morning and crust in the night
Be like a babe unintending in the must
Babe in sight without blasting in the mind
Minding and meandering despondent
in the wings of resign
Begin belonging, addressing, reserving in the Now
Bathe in loving wonder
Abide to become tender miracles
from here on Now

INSIDE

Fastidious times are yet to come
Show us how to live our harms
Within us is the answer Now
Remaining present to the end of time
Deserving all there is to be sown
Lingering in this sea of calm
For we are the true Divine
Who shows us what is fine

CHAPTER 5

SELFLESSNESS

According to countless reasons why we are able to be selfless is one that rings true to me and you may agree that when we are comfortable in our own environment, although it may be constantly at change, we blossom and can become wholly selfless through service and gratitude.

Gratitude to me is an important factor in life. It seems to me that when we are grateful our blessings multiply. I have experienced this first-hand and continue relating to this sublime and great feeling of contentment as we reach a place where being thankful for all that we have right now is just exactly what we need. When we are in such a gratifying space where we accept, acknowledge and behold all that is dear to us and all that we have accomplished till this moment and have held ourselves high in satisfaction of being here, we contend with a vast amount of selflessness.

This truth being voiced is the beginning to self-awareness in perpetuity. We continue to strive as spiritually evolved people when we can and do become selfless at no cost. It is true that this could pose problems but problems are sometimes created by us, it seems; for that matter I'll share some with you. We think in this fashion because we may have suffered consequences after exposing our selflessness nature. In any case, we can continue to be that which we are, as I mentioned earlier, at no cost, as it is a worthwhile state for us to feel the overwhelming goodness that comes to us in many forms. One of these forms by which I receive, is the blessing of contentment when I share with everyone in my life and that feeling is so intrinsically satisfying and benevolent that I wish to continue experiencing this God-given emotion and apply it to my living forever.

When we give of ourselves we are sometimes taken for granted and when we don't receive similar treatment we are offended and may stop giving unconditionally because we were hurt. When expressing "giving unconditionally," I extend to say that it is whole-hearted love we give and need not keep it from spreading it to the whole wide world! We encompass this universal attribute in all that we do with lightness of heart and when we do, we empower ourselves and keep our own light shining bright. In keeping light-hearted and selfless we encounter great rewards of kindness, appreciation, love and for sure, unconditional wealth of these. Our potential to become selfless is so great and we need not worry about outcomes. We need to continue our service.

Everyone is here for a reason. We may not know the reason but everyone in the Universe has reason to be. We are here to grow and develop and use all our potential for the goodness of mankind. True, we deflect and lose our course at times but when we are within ourselves we can reap countless benefits and those are free-falling for us and are accessible at all times if we so wish it to be. Stop trying to tell yourselves not to be like this or like that! Go with the flow and "Easy Does It". We are meant to flow and don't you think that when we do, we are amazed? Keep on track because whatever it may be that we are persisting on doing is exactly what we are supposed to be doing. Ultimately, if we are doing whatever we think is best for us and who's to say we shouldn't? Be accepting of yourself and stop the self-criticism as well as your own self-judgment. We are just fine the way we are right now. You might agree with me that our yearning is clear. We all want to be loved and we strive for joy. When we give love and joy we automatically receive it in return. We are what we think we are. If we wish to be self-less beings we can and will be. Question yourself why not and you may receive the answer you were looking for because everything I repeat "Everything Is Within You."

In wanting transformation for ourselves we may want to begin by making a written list of attributes which we wish to invoke for ourselves. Maybe a handful would be great for starters. Also write the ones you already own. Not overwhelming ourselves will be an achievable request to our inner-self. Do not be afraid of sharing with your good friends what it is you wish, because just like magic, you shall be blessed and essentially every true friend wants the best for us and they are sometimes the vehicle we need and the conduit from which we receive enormous strength, resilience and support.

EVOKE

Magnified inside
Tumultuous gathering is soon renewed
Withered, battered, electrified
Evident of what is due
Day to day it may not exist
But non-the-less satisfied within
When we are not in shape
Unveiling how the group is heard
Be in touch without regret
And without giving it much thought
Tuning in to inspired desires
And make them become your visions for reliance

END OF TEMPEST

Hope, gratefulness, blessings
Dreams of Forgiveness
Weary of treading turbulent waters
Thankful for the tempest
Transforms into pillars of strength
For the Future of Now
And forevermore

OBLIVION

Sweet release in ecstasy
May well be our desire
See truth and delight
Through our disparate eyes
Believe in the find, stride through
Deserving the blessing that is so hailed
For we then realize that we are awake

CHAPTER 6

ENDEAVOR

One morning when I was in the shower I kept thinking that I wanted to deliver a speech. It started like this: *I have a story:* A story like many of us have: What does your story say? What does your story strengthen or for that matter, what does it weaken? We all have a string of stories that we tell each other. We recount it to our friends, our acquaintances, we even tell strangers at times! I have! We maintain our story because it defines who we are, or we think it does... the ego is clever, so very astute in making us believe what we think. But it doesn't have to be this way! It – being the ego – can be diminished. It can be contained and minimized. It takes effort, continued effort, responsibility and belief in what we are doing to it. If we live our lives in our stories, that is what we do the same – o, same – o, stories to different people that come through our lives – it is endless. It could be pitiful story, it could be a shameful story, it could be a story of courage, one of desperation or even of cruelty, whatever your ego wants to use – that's the story's foundation.

When we are in the heart the story may be the same when told but in the heart, the story does *not* need validation from anyone. When in our hearts the story becomes an empathetic one, one which is told but where *we* don't need anything from telling it, we're telling it for either an unknown reason, a necessity or be it what it may, we don't need to analyze it or why we're telling it, as long as you can let it go and do not seek compassion, love, understanding or anything else for that matter. When we don't seek anything or any desires of being understood, the ego lets go and so does the seeker of things, like compassion, etc. We do not need anything from the outside; we have everything we need within us. We are endeavoring letting go and being in our hearts.

We are born into families all over the world and some of us are brought up with love, understanding, patience, kindness and many good things. At the same time, others are not lucky, if we may call it that because I believe that everything that happens does so for a reason. The reason we're talking about is what you want to make use of it for. Some of us suffer many injustices in families including incest, physical abuse, emotional abuse, mental abuse, hunger, and the list goes on.

Coming back to what I mentioned earlier that everything happens for a reason, it is my belief that we are meant to resolve the issues we are faced with in order to grow and develop. Even when given love which we would think this to be wonderful, it could well cause riffraff in the family, maybe a father, mother or sibling is resentful of love shown to another family member. When we receive abuse, we also need to learn how to resolve it by maybe retracting our closeness to the predator or confronting them or even avoiding them. What I am really trying to impart is: this which happens to us is so that we may resolve the challenge and <u>continue on</u>. In finding a way we not only strengthen our resolve by becoming aware of what we were facing, which is the first step but we also think of a way that might work and thirdly we put it into action and follow through with it. Once the plan is executed, the ball starts rolling and when that happens, we're on a roll. We become stronger because we identified the problem and thought of a solution, created a plan of action and executed it. If the plan fails, we do not give up because life is not about giving up but rather, facing our challenges and misfortunes in a positive and resilient manner. We make adjustments and create another plan of action towards the challenge faced.

Since we develop differently and at a difference level from others, this is why one of the reasons we are not to judge others and compare ourselves with others whether be it because we feel others are inferior from us or even if we think they are superior to us. Everyone is evolving and learning at a different pace and do not share an identical conduit and approach in order to accomplish all we can be.

There seems to be a myriad of obstacles in the way of completing our problem solving. Wouldn't you know? What happens when you resolved an issue and right after doing so we get another one! "Oh My Gosh!" We are terrified, angered, saddened and sometimes overwhelmed. Why, because we thought we had tackled our last problem and decided it was done and that was that. Well you did, and you will need to do this for a long while. Until we are redeemed, we are continually growing and developing and problem solvers until the end of time, it may seem. When the time comes the challenges are received without difficulty and the solving is a mere walk on the beach feeling. Things become easier and easier and that's when we are really living, in the true sense of the word. This is what we came here for; don't ever give up. It is your destiny and you are in charge of it.

Many of us have difficulty in focusing on what we wish to accomplish. In the back of our minds we know we need to lose some weight, eat healthier, stop smoking, stop working so much, and maybe have more time for ourselves. As with everything else, we are continuing to do what we always do. We procrastinate, we talk ourselves out of it, we change our minds, we give up, we feel sorry for ourselves and we keep looping around forever not accomplishing what is important to us. In fact, we know what we want but we are so preoccupied with others, yes, with others and we are so uncooperative and competitive that we do not focus strongly and supersede our desires for success. We do trial and error; we regress and cannot seem to find our way.

For me, discipline of the mind works. Believing in myself in such a comfortable and loving way that I do what I know is good for me. Now, I wasn't always like this. I worked on my issues for a while as we may blame others for our continued disorder but in the end we need to realize that we created our own misery as well as our own reality or bliss. I repeat that we are in control and yet we go off to the wayside.

Discipline and love are somehow connected. When we are strong in the mind (and everyone can be that) we stay on task whatever the circumstance, come rain or shine. We do what we set out to accomplish. In doing so, and when we accomplish our God given goals or task at hand we then feel loved by ourselves and by one and all. We become enthralled in feeling, a wonderful appreciation of that which we do. This becomes you and how you live. By continuing to discipline ourselves our mind undergoes changes which are positive and for our own goodness. We know what is good for us, therefore do not self-sabotage as we sometimes do. Continue strong, decisive, disciplined, it is a great feeling that will serve us well. In reality we are very able beings and we can allow ourselves to achieve what we want in life and what we decide we wish is of our own doing. By strengthening our minds we are able to go forth steady and confident achieving our dreams.

WITHOUT

Beggars we are unseen and unheard
How can we give what we have not earned?
Have no regard for life or self-love
That which we're born with from the start
Keeping without is just what embellows
A want unsatisfied by serve-less fellows
The antidote of what surely we're fired with
And for all of mankind and future to kindle

ACHE

Eager is our desire for living
Depending on the games we play
Deciding, minding, eyeing
A wayward plan may invade
Becomes unknown to us
Restore my faith please do so
Attaining splendor to this day
In all we wish to see today
Our almighty strength is then regained

TURMOIL

A sea-wall is built slowly at an easy pace
For one of these days we'll need to stop the flow
For which we are so needy to sow
The current of turbulence
And learn to be abstain
Of thoughts that bring us much disdain
Tis true we don't intend
To oblige ourselves in this way
So stop the forced current, I say
And bless the time of day

CHAPTER 7

LOVE

They say that love is blind. Well it can be and it's fine. Love can be diminished, it can be contained and minimized just the same as a computer screen window, placed aside for a moment or for the longest time and/or forever – it could be our goal to set, to love and be loved because it is the greatest feeling in the world and our goal to access its intensity! It takes incessant effort, continued strength, responsibility and belief to truly find it.

Balancing our lives with love and laughter is essential to well-being and aliveness. When we are in touch with our inner self and inner child we find peace and acceptance. By experiencing Laughter Yoga we become focused in being ourselves with no judgments of ourselves, we then can easily identify with our innate nature; a true child-like state. Practicing Laughter Yoga benefits our soul, the benefit reaches far beneath our internal organs and when we exercise in this way including the diaphragmatic breathing, we become healthier and gain more unconditional love for ourselves as well as for others. Because we are in the moment and at ease with this practice, we can become immersed in the Now. Gaining the release which is accessible when laughing we involve ourselves in beneficial outcomes such as, losing our inhibitions, relaxing, feeling happy and it also changes the chemistry in our brains. We also become freer and thus become more present at all times even when we are not involved in the laughter but it nevertheless makes us more relaxed and therefore we can be more aware of our own presence and be more aware of "being."

When we can reach into our inner source of strength and resilience through "being" – meaning, being in the moment with who we are, we can truly be happy and love ourselves unconditionally. Imagine loving oneself unconditionally. When we can do this we can then love life infinitely. We can love and accept whatever life brings us even if we don't like it. I believe that much of what happens to us cannot be blamed on circumstances or others. We are ultimately responsible to lead our lives for the highest good if we choose to do so. We also reach decisions which change the course of our lives. Even if we decide something that at the moment seemed erroneous, if we lead our lives in acceptance of ourselves and don't feel like we made mistakes, life will become us and what we do will have meaning at some point in time if not right away.

Knowing oneself and acting responsibly at all times takes courage, strength and resilience and if we maintain integrity in living well without abusing our health and our community we are able to thrive in any circumstance we have created for ourselves. Remembering our innate feeling of wellness is crucial to finding peace and harmony. Once we find peace and harmony within ourselves we won't let it go because it feels divine. The divinity within us is there whether we believe it or resist it. We endure greatness within. Everyone has a beautiful life if we decide to remember the beauty the world brings us. When we look at what's good and great in our lives and become grateful of all and everything, then life is great and good and goodness surrounds all that we do, it is impossible to have fear and doubt if there's innate faith and hope within us. Cultivate these attributes and practice every day. We don't need a lot of outer guidance to do this. Listen to your inner state of being, feel it, own it, enjoy it and love thyself. It will fill your body and soul with immense loving energy which you'll retain forever. Sleep, dream, live, love, laugh and all is good within you.

It is important to learn not to be reactive of sorrowful feelings or become angry at things that which are beyond our control. Doing so will be of no avail to us. Once we become reactive and blame others for our perceived sorrows or circumstances, the mind runs away with itself and there's no harmony. Harmony begins with our own sense of well-being because we "choose" to be well. *We* are in control of ourselves.

We are not alone. As the saying says, "We can get a little bit of help from our friends." Friends may come and go but when you have someone who can be a sounding board for you and can help support you in your quest for understanding why and how things that happen are fine. Friends can be such a good source of light, even if our friends have a different up-bringing or culture from us. They can be a stronghold of love and harmony for us whether we are in turmoil or at peace. Give friends the opportunity to be that. To be a friend and to be a listener of our friend's heart-to-heart dialogue is one of the best things you can do for a human being. To be there and listen to a person that needs a friendly ear is a truly wonderful thing to be. A "seer" can see this. They can see the need of a friend and be there in what that friend needs on a certain day. Talking about listening, it's wonderful to listen to a friend. It could be that this certain friend may turn out to need affirmation that what she or he is gearing up to do is just fine. We could be there at the right moment and we will know what to say, to console, to care, to love, to reciprocate when needed, to support, to be what the other person needs us to be. We are responsible, if we care about humanity, not only to be there, but to try and understand what is needed and give what the other person wishes. It's not for us to give what we want to give. It is up to us to know what is needed. "Look and you shall find". It would be selfish and self-centered of us if we gave what we want to give the other just for our own need or satisfaction. When someone needs us, our needs need to be put aside. We may not know right way, but if we listen carefully, the way words are expressed or if there are tears or anger, frustration, then we can go forward and give what is needed at the appropriate time without jumping into conclusions assessing too quickly of our experience. When we cannot fathom what others are going through it is hard to console or assist. At this point, we may want to empathize with our friend because we don't necessarily know how to support them. All it takes is love. Love is a stronghold for the goodness in life. Love bears no grudge. Love is honest and comes deep from the heart and when we add laughter we manifest more love to ourselves and the people who surround us. Give it up, give it up to all you encounter and entertain it with peace and harmony for as long as you live in love and laughter of one-self.

Being in the present and being in love with all that is good is the best and healthiest way to endure anything that happens, whether you created it or think you did or even think you didn't. Because we all are mainly in our minds, it becomes difficult to maintain the innate state of bliss. When we can be in our hearts more, we'll be able to feel more. Most of us don't want to feel pain that may be why we never get there. "Get there, feel, live, love, laugh". By feeling all there is to feel we can and will be alive in the true sense of the word.

ENDLESS LOVE AND FREEDOM

Right Now Is the Time For Realization
Feeling your spirit soar eagerly
Wondrous Moments Living in the now
Laughing, Loving and Living Fully
Free of sinister worries unknown or not
Air filling our path with gentle Breeze
Breeze in the beach waters
Emerged in the waters of love and life
Belong to the being-ness of being
And live all joy today and in permanence

SPIRIT

Wondrous moments are here to stay

Attracting creation in all our being

Anonymous to us what shall remain?

Keep ever-present and succumb to glory

To what you'll call your will and destiny

Often times we so forget

Assured and anointed are we declared willing?

Believing existence to which we belong

Our adoration and contentment

for eternal love and peace

WONDER

Pristine cisterns do exist
Calming creeks in ravines
External drives and internal wealth
Deriving, seeking, prevailing
Clean ravines where animals breed
Longing for existing peace
Be well, for I am

Chapter 8

ALLOWING

It is of tremendous importance when we enlist ourselves to become more creative, we are using our hidden will to make things happen. Not only are we in the moment but we are becoming one with oneself. It is a wonderful feeling that of creating something out of pure intent. When we create a painting, a piece of jewelry, a knitted item, or anything that we create and start, this begins to open our creative center. This center starts growing and in listening and allowing this part of you to be in touch with creation, it can carry about an inner joy and calm. It's the same as going out for a nature walk, you start by making the decision to go for a walk, then when you actualize your first thought of going for a walk then you act upon it. After commencing your walk you enjoy the movement as well as seeing the scenery before you and other benefits of walk may be the exercise depending on how fast or if you are moving your arms to make it more of a power walk, etc. One thing comes and then the other evolves. We meet new people or people we know on this nature walk, we find a new type of flower we've never seen; we encounter a new feeling of warmth or satisfaction. It all pertains to start with a creation and go with it and it may take you in a direction you had never thought possible of entering, as we are continually surprising ourselves when we use our inner freedom to guide us to endless possibilities.

It is for us to endeavor and to create and not tell ourselves that we are not creative, because every person on this earth is a co-creator. We create love, joy, blessings, self-assuredness, possibilities, ideas, wonderful memories, indispensable relationships. Beginning with the beginning, is to listen to your heart and soul and without thinking that we ought to do this or that and without evaluating why or why not, we need to go forward and be decisive in what we really want in life and believing that we shall be successful. When we believe in that which we're undertaking, it is what brings us enjoyment, release, pleasure, fulfillment and so forth. We are conforming and comforting our thoughts and desires and are saying "yes" to our soul.

Coming back to the thought that we ought to continue loving ourselves and not thinking twice about what and how we truly feel and if we wish to do something in life, we have and deserve the right to be happy if that is what we wish. Now, I have encountered individuals who choose not to be happy. It behooves me to know that unhappiness in an existence is where they want to be. If that brings them some kind of self-acceptance or love, I'm not sure. Misery wants company, so when I've encountered someone who delves in re-counting several sad stories which are not of great sadness as we call it, a very traumatic story but just a small encounter with life's displeasures, then I choose not to involve myself. As I've mentioned earlier, when we involve ourselves with trivialities we set ourselves for the never-ending looping of our minds and our mind governs us then to unhappiness and dissatisfaction. Why not go with what we can do rather than on what life is happening to us and blaming others for their behaviors unto us. The lesson is to avoid seeing that this person did this and why and what for etc. When we are involved with those negative effects of happenings the only way to solve and eradicate this type of displeasures from happening is to see it from a perspective of a lesson. WIIFM? "What's In It for Me?" How can I learn from this? Then seek inside for compassion for the individual you are communicating with for maybe having put you in the fight or flight mode or as I call it, in a frenzy and accept the lesson. We don't know what's happened in this person's day or life. We don't know anything. They may have had someone close that's died suddenly or someone has become very ill or someone that they knew had been tragically murdered. What I'm getting to is that we have the ability to be more compassionate and pardon people for their own suffering and if it trickles down to your own life in different ways, pardon them again.

When someone is in pain, they may not intentionally want to hurt you by making a mistake or conveying something to you that may dramatize you. If at the moment of interaction with them we stop for a moment and think; and end judgment and criticism because of their behavior and stand on a place of equal ground (we all make mistakes and open our mouths and blabber atrocities) and when we don't condemn them, we win. When we win it's a feeling of love and compassion towards the other person, so we are nourishing our souls by the art of being more compassionate and accepting even if we don't fully understand where they may be coming from because for one, we don't know, two, we are not going to become inquisitive, judgmental or critical but we become accepting the individual at face value and how she or he is right now in this moment. By respecting and accepting people how they are, we set ourselves free because we are not concerned and we do not live their lives. We have enough work to do in our own life and lifetime to need to meddle in another's. Accept them, love them and if you have to, leave them and love them as well. They'll continue their journey of lessons which are endlessly unfolding and as I've mentioned earlier, we and only we can take responsibility for ourselves and behave in an upright, compassionate, loving and caring manner, contemplating and observing others without the need to criticize. We may think about the other person's behavior being of poor taste, then again, we haven't walked in their shoes so who are we to say? Love conquers all and with love comes other compassionate qualities like, generosity, acceptance, non-judging, inspiration, motivation and many more specialties we have and can maintain or acquire. This is a purpose we may need to reserve as every day goes by when we learn new ways of being. Being accepting not only frees us but it soothes our soul because when we are accepting of others we are also accepting of one-self; inclusive of all our good qualities as well as with all our flaws.

Love encompasses worldly things. We are such loving beings. We can use this devotion to serve humanity at large and end wars, dislike for other races, or dislike of others who we think are different from us (in our minds – because we are similar). At times we can be cantankerous and when we become stressed for some reason, we become it, it being uncooperative, unaccepting, insensitive, and harsh and the list may be endless!

PATHWAY

Divine is my delay
In which I live by this day
Who knows why this is the way
In which we seek the peace
Which we will find at our own front door within
Because we are in search of our souls' needs
Be patient in all of your waking days
For it's supposed to be
That at the end of this delay
It may support us in a way
In which it's meant to arise
And one that is right for us
And as dear to us and in what we need this day
To surprise ourselves even more than we could say

MIRRORS

Mirrors we are gleaming in each other's lives
Holding on the light for the seer to see
Want not, keep not aware of woes
As surely supposed in efforts of sorts
Belong to the sphere of enormous vast wealth
To become, to behold, nevertheless
Be secure for the love of your soul
In height and in harmony with serenity to hold

FORLORN

Enormous strides are spent every day
Some in truly dire contempt
Please know a new way
Of easing the pain away
Tis not for us to say
Why this is the way
Be it the play of the day
Which we are here to stage
Why not be here in a way
That is more content and sane?

Chapter 9

UNITY

In unison we make our lives resounding with strength, quality and so much more by adhering to the universal understanding that we are all intrinsically woven together like a beautifully crafted mantle. A mantle that keeps us bundled in warmth and fortifies our souls when people of all races and cultures unite in oneness of being. As we have been forevermore connected just as lost pieces of a puzzle and it becomes our duty or our destiny to find the pieces and fit them in place and make ourselves and our lives more in equation with what I call "The mantle of peace and unity."

Have you ever felt how your heart warms and our internal radiance becomes aware of all that is when we congregate with people who we truly care for? Are we aware at every moment why and how this happens? When we connect with others we are supposed to learn something in the same way they are learning from you as well. Have you ever noticed that something you wished for yourself or for someone you care for came to you when you met someone new? I believe that we are interwoven and our needs are met when we cooperate with synergy, love and camaraderie of soul. To understand this marvel is to understand the underlying signs when complete wonder happens and it happens a lot just as miracles do happen daily. I've always desired to have more tranquility and by this I mean being able to sit for longer periods of time and not have to do anything. I've always been, you could say, "On The Go." Being busy and although I've been at peace with myself for a long time, I did desire more quiet and restful time awake. Suddenly, I received this which I wanted. In being surrounded by people who convey peace, tranquility, sound mind, consideration, good learning and things of this sort, I became just like them. It is enlightening for me to know that the goodness I wish for myself God gives me. We ask and pray or wish what we truly want and it happens. Because happenings do develop in miraculous ways I believe that what happens is always for our good and for our eternal being to learn and to adapt ourselves unstopping to the wonder that becomes us. Associate with people who we believe to be a better source of light than ourselves at the present moment. Be and it shall be. Ask and you shall receive. Maintain good faith and peace of mind because with this at your side you'll not need to relinquish that which you've always been a part of the collective soul system that nourishes us and keeps us in great form.

A myriad of people I've come to know and all in all this has been a great opportunity for growth and learning. When we meet someone, I believe we need to ask ourselves what lessons are they bringing us and which fortune this will bring us because as I've related earlier, everything happens for a reason. I can recount so many things that I've experienced and once felt like a victim, as well as I know the old feeling, replaced by a new and non-victimized me. Maybe we need to feel this condition so as to limit their power and to train our minds and learn how to dissolve these unwanted feelings and emotions. Conceivably, I did rid myself of this victim state of mind and relinquished my true soul being that which is smooth and unscathed with the love of mine. I'll clarify. It's to do with our living days, days in and days out and I repeat, "believe, believe, and believe." God, higher power and whatever you believe in puts in our hands what we can make of good use as we well know from the start, that all is well within.

We have become very outwardly seeking personalities and greed has developed slowly. When we don't share what we have, we are taking away from the Divine. Giving and sharing is part of love and unity. How can humanity continue the way, the way of selfish attitudes? Wanting so many things we wish like status, class, makes us who we are not and although some of us attain all that, we still are not content when we've conquered our thirst and still want for more. We need to be thankful for what we have achieved till this moment and not look at our neighbors and want what they have. Being in an internally beautiful place in time will assist us in arriving in peace and letting go of the material world which exists. It seems to me this has been planted for us to either deteriorate in our existence or on the other hand, to force us see the light and join with it. It sounds to me that unrequited possessions are making us heavier instead of lighter, letting go of baggage serves us well; inner baggage as outer baggage as well. We become enslaved to work more, gain more material wealth when in fact; we don't realize that the job of marketing and sales out there is just a way to have us spend our hard earned money. It's useless to continue hoarding and obtaining more materialistic items which seem to be useless often times, and we close our hearts more deeply when we can't afford to buy. Letting go and being contented with what we have, be it plenty or not, in our own eyes we need believe that it's fine without as well as we have everything we need within us. United we ought to live and united we shall need to strive to be so that we can convince ourselves of what a great blessing this would be to realize.

SYNCHRONICITY

Unveil what it's for us to know
And keep it in your quest for soul
For love abounds at every door
If only you shall find the roar
And be it well for us to see
Become united with our palms
Which do not require extraordinary qualms
But sync into the love you are
United with and joined within the higher being

UNION

Motionless as a rock are we
Everlasting, deep and sunken
Planted in earth like a floral beauty
Peaceful place for you and me
Earth, stronghold of love
Undivided within, internally linked

BESTOWED WITH LOVE

Suspended into the sphere of the light
Descendant to the life Within
Consoling heart in pure delight
and harmony in sight
Scribe and serve through Love
Keeping Within as a sign of
clear and precise design
That bases our entire life
With a flowing and glowing mind
Addressing no wounded heart
Love, Love, Love.

CHAPTER 10

GREATNESS

Is everyone's dream. We are the dream, we are awareness, we are beautiful when we believe this to be true, and we are that. Vulnerability is seen as a weakness in today's day and age. When we are vulnerable we are simultaneously powerful and strong. Power and strength begin inside us and is therefore of use and potentiality. Keeping ourselves vulnerable makes us as strong as a mule because when we can be open and show our weaknesses, my goodness, how strong are we? If we are as strong as we believe, we are! Do not underestimate yourself, ever. Believe in yourself and one way you can do this is by not being a good listener to negative comments or negative support, meaning, negative reinforcement of doom or loss or for that matter, doubt. When someone starts ranting negativity towards a belief of theirs, do not react and defend yourself but let them believe in it, but this doesn't mean you need to accept their points or beliefs. <u>You are the believer of your dreams.</u> Ponder on this fact and become in love with what you want to do in life even if it's not clear yet. Belief is major in our lives and we can only believe what we desire to hold in our belief system whether it is a large thought with plans and goals or if it's a way of thinking to the best of our beautiful nature. Do not allow breakdown in your beliefs, whether they are heart-strong ones or baby-step ones. You are their owner and thus you are the believer and believe is what you shall do. Become united with them and set free your soul.

When we are without internal power, I would say we are without. Being without can cause a lot of imbalance and deter us from achieving our goals and dreams. Internal power to me, is understanding one's own ideas, talents, wants and needs. When we know what we want and having achieved and executed our internal power we set forth a wheel and when this happens we become like we say "On A Roll." The more you do something the more you can do it and the more you do it, the better you become at doing whatever you've decided to pursue. If you pursue happiness, you'll reach contentment, if you ask for love, you'll receive it and of course first you need to give it! When you are in your own power, what this means to me is that we do not need anything from the outside world. Our innate power is one with us and cannot be taken away or lost. Its strength could subside in times of distress but never gone for we have everything we need inside of us. As I express "Everything Is Within Us and Without Us."

By saying that we have everything we need inside of us, I don't mean we can do it all on our own. We are in this world and of this world and if we are to grow and develop we are going to need many things. The most important thing in my mind is relationship. Relationships: to mother, father, sister, brother, lover, friend, neighbor, cousin, aunt, uncle and friend to yourself. We do not thrive alone. Who thrives alone? No-one! In the end, one who wonders alone, lives alone is without. Without, I mean with no-one to support and in turn, no-one to support them either. Being alone shows me that we have lacked in learning to adapt to others. As we well know, everyone is different and inherently unique. Because of this uniqueness we may well not get along with our sisters and our brothers and everyone we meet along our journey, as well. When we decide to connect and see everyone with eyes of love that is when we'll prosper. Prosper in many ways, other than wealth of riches and financial status. We will flourish as a people when we can (and we can). Observing our neighbors and not finding and telling everyone you come into contact about their faults! We are at fault when we judge, criticize, minimize, affect, diminish and restrain others with our attitudes and attitudes which deny support to any of us. When finding fault is much of what we do, we fail. In my eyes, we fail when we don't unveil the beauty within ourselves and if we did, we are able to see the beauty in others as well. We are a beautiful, beautiful species. We are so well-built and humanly attractive. Everyone has beautiful features. Everyone has beautiful eyes. Look at people's eyes and when you make contact and view the beauty within, you will be amazed. I repeat, have no fear for fear is just a delusion of the mind. Find and you shall seek.

Going back to what I mentioned earlier, the more we find positive things about each other and about the world-at-large the more room for growth. I believe that with self-acceptance first, we are surely to follow with acceptance of others. Why fight, argue, demean, discredit, denounce, and fool ourselves and others? Why would this be an encouraged habit of ours? Delight in goodness, love, love of mankind and become whole and when we become whole we determine how good our lives will be, because our lives are always good. When we accept this concept, how cannot we flourish?

Intrinsically bound by nature's raft we are within ourselves most of the time. At times as I've mentioned earlier, "We Lose It," and when we do, don't fret, just get back in balance and carry on. Continue living without false hope, imagined truths, as well as imagined failures because our species does not fail what we do is like I mentioned earlier, we lose focus. What we need to learn is how to regain our strength and continue on and live a fruitful and courageous life which we all can do and are entitled to by our own choice and not being a victim of our own dissatisfaction.

LOOK

Love is a contemplation of the Divine
This being said is a sure sign
Of what we live by day in and day out
With great significance and sound of mind
Reduce baggage and decrease resistance
Because anew we'll receive persistence
All one deserves and needs to bind
And reserve a well full of peace of mind
Look and you shall find
A deep river of constant design
And live the love of life in mind

SIMPLICITY

Simple treasures abound
Mother Nature, Surrogate Love
Unending bliss for evermore
Entwining in the abyss
Of external fascination with Divine experience

FORGIVE

Wallowing in the rapids of tumultuous times
Engaging, forgetting, awakening
Sentence without; dreams abound within
Serenity, Allowing, Moderating, Loving

Chapter 11

HEART

Laughing with our hearts wide open makes us freer and at times more vulnerable. When we are laughing we are in the present moment. Being in the moment is important because it gives the mind a break from perpetual thinking. Using laughter as a benefit towards lightness is invigorating for the body and mind. It is a well-known fact that "Laughter is the Best Medicine." Not only does it release the stress we keep in our bodies but it allows us to survive in times of distress. We become serious, so serious that we don't live fully the way we are innately supposed to. By becoming lighter during the total amount of our breathing lives and by creating laughter and lighten our atmospheric region or space, we create a better, more peaceful arena for ourselves and others by supporting lighthearted accounts in our existence and become less inhibited and more alive.

Numerous people in the arts have brought laughter in our lives. My Godmother, Sarah, may she rest in peace, adored Victor Borges, why, because listening to him play the piano and sing and make people laugh was such a beautiful and splendid feeling for her as I recall her telling me about him and laughing while she spoke. Wishing for a beautiful feeling, there is one sure way to bring about more joy into our lives and that is to sing, dance, be merry and laugh. Research has shown that if we laugh for no reason, the benefits are the same as if it was real. As I mentioned earlier, endorphins are released and the same as "Runner's High" we become joyful and it feels good. Why not feel good? Sometimes we are living and identifying with pain and struggle and that's all we know. I believe that even if we can't let go of this type of identification we can at least try to give it up and transcend it. We human beings are able to do anything we set our minds to, if this is what we wish to do. There are no limitations but only the ones we decide to inflict on ourselves. Truly, it's difficult to do things we may think we cannot do, but deep down when we desire the intent of growing and developing ourselves for the highest good, we can and will evolve with more joy. It takes time – a lot of time to do this. Know that time is of the essence. We know when it's time to do something we've all wanted to do all our lives. Like for example; I've always wanted to be in movies, so this winter I'm ready to enroll in a theater class at my local college. It's taken me some time even from the moment I decided to want to do this but it's taken a year for me because I had other priorities which I wanted to accomplish before. One of my priorities was writing this book. This book had been a thought about ten or more years before it came to fruition. I started writing it in the Summer of 2011 and finished it in the Winter of 2013. I lived, learned and slowly determined and wished to write a book before becoming a motivational speaker. What I'm saying is: what we all know and have heard before and this is: we are able to put our thoughts and dreams to work, whatever it is that we desire, we can and will do so. The ability to create is within us and it's up to our own consciousness to go ahead and become who we really are and what we came here to do. I say "Find It," find that which fulfills you, find it, own it and keep it. Keep it but at the same time, give it away, for we are meant to share the goodness which we feel and own and offer it with love.

LIVE TRULY

Sifting through the light of day
How do we pretend the stay?
Wishing how to make it through
Tis what we wish to do
Feigning, frowning forcing through
Why are we so tempted to
Withstand the lies of today?
Not for our souls to hearsay
The abounding truth we fear
Be safe, be sound and dutifully do
Uphold and hang in the untimely thrash
Be strong, be heard, be known and be well
Because at the end of time
All will suffice

BELIEF

Be like muscle memory
Keeping the great feeling aware
Being fair to ourselves
May be all we need to fare
For we are the mystery
With which we shall succeed
And believe that true confidence
Is constantly at ones hands
We shall then succeed truly
When we so instill belief
And lift, lift, lift

FUTURE

It is a reverie of mine
To walk with a glowing plan
Without despondency and above all
Without tremors or fright
But full of delight
And in search of the light

Chapter 12

TRUTH

It is believed that the truth hurts! Why is it that this is perceived so? Could it be because we don't want to see our faults? Maybe one of the reasons of seeking truth is becoming who we need to be, more conscious and aware as well as more respondent to others, more assertive in our ways and what we need for ourselves first and then pay it forward to others? The truth speaks for itself. No-one has to state the truth because deep down, we know it. We know it so well that if it's not pleasant, we hide it! Bring it out, all of it, don't let it wither and die, bring it out and use it to transform for that is what we are born to do. Who was born knowing all? Everyone learns, we all choose what we want to know whether it be directly or indirectly learned or acquired or through birthright, we do have some traits and genetic information stored in our dna but ultimately, we need to use what we got as well as learn what we don't have, put it together and transform ourselves for the better for mankind's sake.

Sure, it's easy to rest on our laurels and not do much but isn't it a good feeling to push ourselves to do what we think we cannot? Yes, to do what we think we cannot is true transformation. If we can do this, we can tap into our innate endless potential as love is endless potential. To become the master of our own divinity is to have desired love, health and well-being for mankind. If each one of us chooses to strive and grow and develop spiritually, what a great way to live. Wanting to recognize, feel and not fight our emotions? Be it what it may. "I Say, Go For It." And whatever makes you tick, without looking back to the way it used to be. Be a wholesome person, growing in love of life and in love of the wisdom we have attained for the highest good. Do not fear. Fear hurts. Be not afraid. When once I was asked, "What do you fear?" I replied, "I fear of finding a fear." Have faith in your being and you shall be sustained. Be a stronghold of courage and internalize faith, for without faith life cannot be lived in the fullest sense.

Be in your truth – no one else can live your truth. Within us lies the innate truth of our existence. When we are real to ourselves we are happy. When we are being someone we are not, we are without. Sometimes we feel different emotions such as inaptitude; inadequacy, jealousy, envy and the list may go on. When we are feeling in some way wanting of something, it could be a material possession, a status in life or even a feeling of being loved, needed and desired, whatever feeling we may have may arise at different stages of our lives. It is imperative that we identify this feeling and deal with this emotion. When we do not deal with our emotions and brush them under the carpet, as I've mentioned earlier, emotional mildew arises. This trapped emotion becomes occult and heavy; this may be called our shadow. Dealing with feelings and emotions according to my beliefs and experience is having cognition of ones-self, in other words, knowing ourselves. We all want to thrive and be successful in life and we are comparing, desiring others' possessions, wanting what is not ours to get. There are myriads of examples, you get my gist! By loving ourselves first and acknowledging our flaws and impairments we begin to experience the truth. When we see our weaknesses and go onwards to develop a stronger self by being aware of it, we grow in brilliance.

Inexplicably for me, it is an essential internal requisite for a joyful existence. Imagine living with a loveless feeling for oneself. How can we succeed in feeling well when we brush away all the flaws we could be working on? By not disentangling our emotions and ridding ourselves of fear, we waste precious time. Just as we were in a maze, we can get to the other side but it might take us much longer. Become aware of your own self. This is your sole purpose to resolve and go on. Others will do or won't do the same. Beware of your daily thoughts and feelings because they are a roadmap to the needed work of your life to grow, progress and enrich your own being. By elevating your own being you are consequently elevating everyone in your path who wish to absorb the richness, joy and light that is emanating from within you. When you are without in the world your sole goal is to go within and trust your own being; it will not betray you, others may. Blessings are to be received daily and miracles also are received when we open ourselves to love and become true to ourselves first, then we shall thrive.

SUCCUMB

Splashing water on my face
Even if surrounded in dire straits
Refresh, renew and re-do
This which causes us much ado
And behave in a beautiful way
Everlasting and here to stay

AVAIL ONE-SELF

Immensely based and naturally designed
To serve the world and humankind
This vast pool of Divine Love
To bathe and to soothe
A device which leans toward you too
Inducing love and producing airs
Of much wanted fares

FACING

Encounter returned faith

Above all that is safe

Belong to it and immerse

In a sea of wealth

For it is for us to see

As well as for us to be

Engulfed in its safe-haven

And join in its great returns

Chapter 13

EMPOWERMENT

Using our God-given intellect is being self-empowered. When we are in our truth and remain so, we empower ourselves and remain strong and at ease. Because we remain at ease with our own knowing we are then able to become confident. Confidence, in turn brings, self-respect and assurance that all is well and it is. Our intellect is a very important tool which if not used, stagnates and leaves us without power. Power in ourselves to me means having the knowledge of what it is that our own power will bring us and therefore using this will keep us well and in balance. When we are not empowered and we are not using our intellect we are giving up something which belongs to us for a reason. Having the wisdom to use our intellect and to live well with our own decisions and at the same time is to invoke desired and needed strength to keep ourselves on course. When we feel in our hearts what we truly wish for ourselves and do become positive that what we wish will manifest, we are held up by our higher self. If we are living our reality by going back and always looking into our experiences in certain areas and especially when we are deciding not to change our way of thinking and opening our hearts, we are obstructing what we really want and making ourselves remain unhappy because we are enlisted and decided to live by our usual perceived reality.

It is vital to allow for change. With change, I mean change of heart and change of mind. When we release old patterns of being and wish to bring our desires to fruition, that is true manifestation of the Divine plan and one which brings us love, faith, hope and in the end, peace. Not allowing ourselves the gift of changing our hearts and minds leaves us in disarray and we continue to propagate for ourselves what we don't want. When we think of what we don't have, what we don't want and what we can't get, guess what? We do not attain because our minds have made up this obstacle. I say, kick down the walls that we build, knock them down and visually and mentally view them falling and disappearing. To accomplish this fete, we need strength of mind and purpose together with instilled belief that we can and will attain our peace when we ultimately believe in ourselves and reach within.

Reaching within is all that we are to do daily in keeping our self-love intact. When we love and have respect for ourselves we become so entwined with our own true reality and this self-love brings us joy and contentment of the heart which then makes us have a peaceful existence. With peace comes tranquility of mind and with tranquility of mind comes introspection and we can then contemplate our own behaviors and patterns and maybe bring about a desired change, a positive change that we can re-create peace for ourselves once more.

Now, without discipline this task becomes impossible. We cannot bring about change without discipline. As I have said earlier, "Everything Is Within Us And Without Us." We make choices every day of our lives from the minute we wake up. Small choices, big choices, good choices, bad choices, important choices and every kind of choice there is to be. The reality is that when we choose irresponsibly we lose our discipline and that is when we end up without. What I mean by this is that we have everything inside of us and we too have the choice to not have what we want and then this is without. Because we have not yet realized our innate potential we are afraid of failing or maybe of failing in the eyes of others. We then don't go forward, retract in our path and we lose our belief in ourselves. Because we become undisciplined in our thought process, we subdue ourselves to our lower selves and diminish our own strong desires and end up not attaining our dreams. Do not punish yourself and grieve at this loss of reality which keeps us not transforming into our higher selves. Keep in check with yourself and if you need to write down some goal planning and set some points for yourself so that you may have more discipline and responsibility emerge as strong-points for yourself, do so in a way that is good for you.

We have the necessary intellect to become all that we wish to be. To change and transform is one of our most important challenges. Without change we bring repetitive and uncontrolled situations, when we are replicating the same patterns of living. When we change our thoughts we change our lives. We can have a blessed and positive change in our lives and receive the blessings of richness of the heart because to earn real richness is to attain this state of mind when the material world is seen immaterial of exactly this and we can then be content with nothing of worldly meaning such as objects of material worth and of desire and that which keeps us chained and at times do not serve us well.

Keep walking saintly on, without acquiring so much materialism which we are in constant watchful state through the media and so forth and we wish to acquire the same things which our neighbors have. By asserting ourselves and choosing a different path, we empower ourselves even more. Ask yourself if you need the item or if you want the item. If the answer is that it wouldn't be necessary for your good living, abstain from obtaining because often times we buy too many things that are not of much use. I'm not saying we ought not buy things because surely, our economy needs some revival but what I'm getting at is that we like to use and enjoy what we buy but it might not be put to good use. To use our intellect well and hopefully empower ourselves is to choose what we need and what we don't need and not waste resources on things that are immaterial to us and to the idea that keeps us bound to what is illusion which only makes us feel momentarily gratified.

Haven't you felt how instant gratification works? We suddenly feel this void or need and we decide in our mind that we need to purchase something? Then we get it and feel great. How long does this good feeling last? Is it worth feeling good for a certain part of the day, week or month or longer? Do we wish to feel good only for part of our journey or do we wish to feel great at all times of our waking life? We need to let go of materialism that doesn't serve our spiritual center. Our center needs love and attention and who better can give this to ourselves but our own selves? Yes, remind yourself daily how beautiful you are and how beautiful your family is and how beautiful your friends and neighbors are. We are blessed with people around us. We create our own environment and when we change our minds for the positive and use our intellect for our higher choices we win and then unfold the vastness of love, faith and hope in ourselves forevermore.

Do not own fear because fear is an illusion of the mind. Love yourself with all your might and don't cause yourself unduly fright because we have everything within us and therefore are a stronghold of power, love and resilience.

THE FORGIVEN

Behind us and in front of us
Lies what we are to do
Feelings are soon forgotten
In this day of compassion
Rely on your worldly feelings
Rely on what feels good
Instead of denying the obvious
And in turn going back on your word
Be here and be present
Be able to forgive
For it is due in this time of trouble
Dismount your high horse
And ask yourself for your own forgiveness
And we shall shine again
In forgiveness to others in forgiveness of ourselves

WINGS OF LOVE

Albeit in oblivion searching the days
When one is receiving unending blessings array
Within us is everything and without us as well
Wellness for us exists as pardoning too
Because of rough weathers which we cannot undo
Appearing with thanks is receiving in truth
We are within and without, surely we are
Endeavoring, reflecting, transcending this love
Love which feels peaceful to him and to her
Love is the key be it yours or someone's
Do feel it suspend us in higher command
Address it, conserve it, and mandate it with ease
Unquestionable blessing well worth to receive
Seemingly worthwhile for all of mankind

TRANSFORMATION

It is a travesty of mine state
How I'm withstanding the living days
Wish for, want for, is inapt
The course is set in certain ways
Without having much shame
Tending to wayward ways
Reversing the sting of travesty
We can refine our stay
In this revolving stage which is
Our limited days in this Universe, I say

Chapter 14

RESOLVE

Awareness of the mind, body and soul is an intrinsic attribute to realize as it is of immense value in ascertaining what we need as a being whose purpose in life needs to be unveiled. If we are at all connected to our self-empowerment and that is what we need, we are then able to manifest all the good things we wish for ourselves and the world-at-large. Like a seed which is planted, it is sown and later on the seed catches and it grows into plentiful abundance, the same we could say is with our learning. We are created like sponges able to absorb a lot of information which will avail us of a lot of wealth of understanding. When we do not admit these within us, it becomes voided and discarded as waste product we might say. The absence of real mindfulness is an undetermined source of lost opportunities for creative ideas and education for our souls. When we ignore our intuition believing that it cannot be, we are disregarding our divine potential in assessing life and the conduits surrounding us in order to receive many given blessings and guidance. Do not ignore these! Be more cognizant of messages which come to us for our own growth and development and don't keep on by the wayside ignoring true innate intuition which we all possess. When we ignore this said intuition, this is when we are without. Without support, love, understanding, communion, and it's when fear and doubt emerge. Be of the understanding that we are like students of this plane, here for a reason, here and now in all the sense of the word. Now, here, present and centered. When we begin to be absent we lose quality of thought and when we lose this, havoc abounds.

Let's say for example, that we could identify the world as a vast circus. Everyone in this circus is performing an act. We as observers have the unique power to ascertain the situation that which we are observing. Imagine there's a circle and in the heart of the circle, planted is your person. When looking at the acts in the circus, the circus being your own world whether it be large, small or immense, as each of us has our own company of friends and so forth. When we ourselves are doing our own act, we may pretend, forget, become oblivious, put ourselves in danger, make outbursts, rely on others and the list of irresponsibility could be endless. As I mentioned earlier, we become absent and cannot see the "Act" as I explained and have lost the gist of the story or in other words "What's going on around us." By being absent, I mean, is being lost and out of touch primarily with oneself and then this translates into lost to the world around us and that which could and would be of support to us. By being in oblivion we lose and we've lost a lot. Much of it is lost time but energy is lost together with time because we are like a wheel, turning and turning and not getting anywhere! We are swimming upstream without knowledge and at the same time we are blaming everyone in the stream's path for our mistakes, misgivings and it spoons unrest in our beautiful souls.

Better listen to our minds' chatter and condense thoughts that are not serving us and speak to our higher being. We have several levels of being. Don't you just love being in love? Why the question again? Because love matters! Love is the answer and the answer is written on the invisible wall we're staring at! Don't question it – give love and you shall receive love and all is well and will continue to be. Getting off-center is something we are constantly doing and this is ongoing and unpleasant for us as well as our family and circle of friends. It's important to have support a system and someone whom we may confide in and share any worries or concerns. When we find a person, friend, counselor, doctor or anyone who has love for us and wants to be there for us, we can and will become open and by being open, I believe, it saves us a lot of suffering. We need to listen first to ourselves, then to our needs: there are many. In order to be able to select which needs to attend to and why, we do so by focusing on the bare necessities of life first for example: a job, income, food, home, friends, then when we have these we go on looking and searching for that which we desire, be it peace of mind, more wealth, more love, anything that you focus on, you shall attain.

Same as a person who is always worried and thinking of his or her low financial assets – guess what – the circumstance will remain the same as "What you sow, you reap." If we are focusing on positive reinforcements, love, new things to do, opening ourselves to new opportunities in life we are open to living a desirous and fulfilling life. Try it, you'll like it. Enjoy yourself as it's later than you think. Haven't you heard the elders? They know it well. They say "Where has the time gone?" Whilst we are in this planet, stay focused, dream and when you dream, dream of immense satisfaction. Have lots of love to give and lots of understanding to want to receive. One way you may receive more of what you want is by meditating daily. Madhu, a good friend of mine back in 2009 encouraged me to meditate even if it was just for five minutes upon awakening in the morning and five minutes before going to sleep at night. These times of the day and night are the best times to meditate as proven scientifically. It is when the brain is more open to newness and at bedtime before we go into restful RAM sleep. Meditating has benefitted me enormously and hence I have realized one of my dreams, the writing of this book.

ENCOUNTERS

Encounter returned faith

Above all that is safe

Belong to it and immerse

In a sea of wealth

For it is for us to see

As well as for us to be

Engulfed in its safe-haven

And join in its great yields

SCATTERED

Ranting and raving do we steer
Running up and down the swell
Without stopping at the well
Wishing for a saint address
Where we could find undress
Respite and find release
And space it up with much peace

HOLDING ON

Beknownst to me I have erred
Erred and erred and erred and erred
Please do not mind my way
I know it well but can't accept
All of my unruly reigns
When can't become won't, it is of regret
Because it may seem there's no tomorrow
Holding on to so many things
That which will hold us chained
To ideals we know well
And those which do not serve us well

CHAPTER 15

YOUTHFULNESS

One of the life's fascinations is trying to retain freshness in our lives and something we all relish. Like children, who are mostly in the moment and when in the presence of nature they exist so free and so happy and undisturbed most of the time. It's natural for children to be in an elated state of mind maybe until they start being pulled away by the havocs of restraint that grown-ups impose on them persistently in the hopes that they will grow into responsible and productive adults. We uphold this way of thinking and believe it's good for them. I believe that it's necessary to let children grow at their own pace rather than push them onto a reality that is not for them to persevere and live by. There is plenty of time to grow up and for sure, we ourselves also need to grow up because we don't need to be a child forever as some of us do continue this practice. Of course, it's important for our children to learn responsibility as this is an important and essential part of growing into adulthood. What is also important, in my view, is to let them be. Offer them sufficient time by themselves and ample time enjoying friends. Also allow them time to be a child and not ask them to do adult responsibilities or work so much. This is important as a way to keep them where they are at and it's called "childhood." Experiencing beautiful childhood memories and enjoying their own journey will carry them healthy and sound through the different stages of their lives and into their valued adulthood. When childhood is interrupted by suggesting adult activity it spoils their growth. As children, they need to cherish all that comes along with childhood and levity as well as freedom and joy regularly.

It is great to be like a kid in many ways, we in turn have responsibilities and a careers, occupations etc. which we need to tend to, but what I'm talking about is to be like a kid especially the same as with our inner childlike-state which consists of undertaking what is presently happening and constantly staying in a creative state of mind. Have you observed children? They come up with the funniest ideas!

Have you noticed that young-hearted adults are like youngsters? Young to me means "First stagers." But youngster could be an older person who is free of worry and seriousness. Children and youngsters are laughing, telling jokes, playing, investigating new opportunities and are very open. On the other hand, some adults may be more serious, prejudiced, worried and the list goes on! Why not be like children. Enjoying the moment and keeping young at heart? There's plenty of time to take care of business and this we do. We work outside the home, we keep our homes in good shape and we live. This is fine, to be at work and be serious. How we may be better off is if we aren't in this state all of our living moments! We need to find time to cherish the moment like youngsters do. They are full of life and curiosity, don't be shut down – be like them who are free-folding. Support them in their growth and development in maturing and still allowing them enjoyment in their youthfulness and preserve them young. They will get old like us but at least they know how it feels to be young and free and therefore be able to contain this feeling during their entire lives when they can enjoy their childhood without so much seriousness we grown-ups impose on them at times.

I've come to observe some of our elders who are walking faster than our youngsters and I call them "New-agers." They are amazing! They are in love with life and all its charm and leading a healthy and satisfying life. When we become interactive with groups, organizations, friends, family and anywhere where we are connected, the benefits for youthfulness become trifold. We become happier and healthier beings because we are living in the moment of what the day brings us. We can and will plan ahead though, there's no harm in that but if we can keep in the moment as much as we can it will certainly bring us peace and joy.

No-one is perfect and we will never attain perfection but we can all strive to better our ways consciously and become more responsible for the things that we can do to develop and build connections with other people who are doing just this and continue our journey in a splendorous way, because we can.

CONTINUING SEARCH

Continuing the struggles of our feared life
Hang in, withhold, and search inside your soul
Loving soul comfort, full of love and life force
Destiny, Abundance, Embracing, Wishing
Full of light, vitality and splendor

OPEN UP

Finite, assumed infinite
Open up to love
Fill yourself of it
Ending the closed doors forever
Hugging yourself and
Climbing the staircase of your
imposed infinite love sustained
And thrive

DISCOVER

Richness is not solely a monetary result
But all that is lived with Love and insight
To have and to hold a better reprieve
And a quality of which we might want to receive
Beware of the ploys that we may ponder on
For without what it is that may find us at ease
We may well be deceased in our life of peace

Chapter 16

ORDER

It's vital to uphold and persevere in our own strength, keep trust for ourselves with love and in doing so, what we first need to be accepting of one's fortune or misfortune as sustained in our minds even if we don't understand what our path is, and why we are doing whatever we're doing. The main idea is self-acceptance in all that we are continuously creating and taking in mind that we are keeping order. When I say "order" It means that we are in touch with the feeling that brings about the action, the action being the way we lead our lives. For example, we are to be in love with ourselves first to be able to enjoy our own life. Until we reach complete self-acceptance we cannot and will not be able to love unconditionally. This does not mean that we think so highly of ourselves in the sense and we do not progress in our need to change and learn new ways or that we know it all and have no more need to develop and grow nor does it mean that we have arrived and have reached eternal peace and harmony. But this is the first step for self-recognition and therefore by accepting ourselves primarily, we reach the moment where all that we're doing is in order right now at this certain moment. By understanding our actions and not being harsh on any of our wrong-doings we are cultivating truth in our existence. When we live by our truth, order in our lives begins to flourish. We do not necessarily need affirmations or validation from outside because that would be, in my mind, irrelevant to me. What I'm saying is, believe in yourself in totality. Even if we see that we are erring at times, there is always the chance to fix it; we then regain order in our truth and live with good morals which in turn creates harmony and bliss.

Now, first things first and going back to accepting ourselves being the basis of self-recognition we fortify our inner true identity because there then is no doubt, fear, jealousy and anything of the sort that which would make us not be centered. When we are centered we are in harmony, when we are in harmony it is a delightful feeling and we live for the wonder of feeling delighted. When we feel wonderful because this is what our true nature upholds, we extend it to others. Others receive how you feel and they use it for their own purpose or not. If they are happy and contented individuals they may accept your good vibrations but maybe, if they are people who are decided upon being miserable then they will not receive the good vibrations but when receiving they are converting it in however they wish to feel it. It is not important to us how others perceive us or how others react to us. What is essential to remain unscathed from sometimes the brutality of life and go on giving warmth, love, kindness and extending happiness to our brothers and sisters. We are born with the innate ability to be happy and contented and therefore it is in our true nature to support and keep this feeling no matter what.

Yes, we want everyone to be happy and when they do not want this, it is ok. They choose, we choose, it is ultimately our choices that bring about who we are in the end for better or for worse for ourselves and humanity in all that we do, as we are globally united whether we like it or not. We are who we are we say, we are in all the sense of the word. We are what we act, we are what we eat, we are what we choose, we are just are what we uphold and it is not for us to judge and recommend our ideals onto others. True, we can talk about the things that hold true to us, we can share our ideas with others, that is fine but as I've mentioned before, we do not meddle with people's decisions pushing our own agendas thinking we ought to tell them how to live their lives because their lives were given to them to live from their own hearts and to cultivate it, spread it and maintain it, that is: their love and life's eternal source of light. Each of us knows this very well inside of us and we need not intrude in their lives and actions whether we believe they are wrong or could do better. It is for them to implore for themselves which way to go, for that is the test or may I say; that is what we came here for, to live and learn. Our actions and reactions tell who we are.

I myself will react negatively at someone's comments unknowingly. Most of the time I catch myself soon because I asked for more awareness recently and mind you, we get what we ask for. We may not get it right away, it may take years to achieve things we always wanted but we ultimately reach our goals, destinations and dreams come true if we believe. I repeat that it took me about ten years to write this book but I didn't start writing it until two and a half years ago. My inner intention was that I wished to write a book. I mentioned it at times because I felt it was alright for me to be able to express my desires. I remember a friend saying to my then teenage daughter, "If your mom says she's writing a book, she's writing a book." These words of hers were never forgotten to me. Somehow this mention of hers instilled faith that I was to write a book. Ten years ago I did not know what the book would be about but I knew I wanted to write it. My yearning was heard; I woke up at 4 a.m. and started writing it. I even remember back in the summer of 2008 when another close friend asked me after she heard me mention my desire for writing; she asked what the title was going to be and right off the bat the answer came out of me simultaneously as she spoke the question and I answered her "Unremitting Solace." I didn't know what and how and when but internally I knew the title even though I started writing it three years later. This is why I am sharing that we do not always achieve what we desire right away but when we are inspired by someone or we are inspired ourselves to act somehow what we want becomes creation because we believe we are capable of fulfilling our wishes and dreams and we are all co-creators together.

I believe that our loved ones wish for us what we desire for ourselves and our good friends also wish for our own goodness and that's how the world goes around with good and well wishes from others to create and maintain a system of order, order which maintains peace, love for oneself and the world and that which makes us whole and at peace and everyone has this inside of them if we only dig deep to find and retrieve it for our divine living.

CHANGE

Powered by the light of pure dismay
In gazing at our disorderly ways
Why is this trend here to weigh?
Phase it out and bat it far away
Find out why it's not a worthy stay
And have appreciation for a choice
As soon as you decide to change
It may well be what you've yearned, yesterday
And finally accept as a fine recourse
For our disdain is great, if we don't
amend our unkind ways

ARRIVE

Broken hearts and broken minds
Stumbling around like babes in the dark
Be aware where to stare and reminisce in the air
For today all is fair and is serving us no-where
Portraying unawares of sciences and affairs
That won't weather our prayers
Release and Relax into Love and Resilience
And in that which is destined to
arrive in such brilliance

ANSWERS

We have richness within us
A lighthouse of peace and love
Why do we so want?
Despite of what all we have
Cannot we decide?
Is it difficult to accede?
Our plan is Divine
Within us stands the answer
Question yourself and you'll realize
How much within we have

CHAPTER 17

GRATITUDE

Support and friendship is one of the things that keep us well. Appreciation and understanding of basic human nature is the key to the acceptance of our lot in life. When we are thankful we receive a great feeling of joy and satisfaction. Be in a space where we can recognize the blessings that we have already received and thank the Universe for giving us everything that we need now and continue the journey in a blissful manner.

Gratefulness is so rewarding to the inner self. We are bound to find people along our path that we connect with and they make us happy. I have the good habit of continually thanking everyone whom I encounter because really, everyone we meet is for our good. We all have suffered countless struggles as you may well commiserate with me. These so called challenges are part of living. The recompense is to stride on fearlessly whether or not you think it is a worthwhile project to continue whatever you are aiming in accomplishing.

Being grateful for our existence can multiply the joyful feeling of having everything and therefore becoming whole.

Make a habit of re-constituting a list of all the people you come across. During my lifetime I have made this list and I acknowledge those who have presented many challenges for me and forgiving them is the key to our own wellness. When we gratify people's inequities we release any wrong-doing in their part. We need to continue a positive self-talk so that we may strive in retaining a great living because we were born to do so. Also make a list of those who have given you love, support and understanding, these are also to be kept in high regard as I have mentioned many times before, it is all for our goodness.

I am so very thankful for my family, my friends, my employers, my past friends, my co-workers, my home, my finances, my body, my health, my God-given attributes and talents, my destiny, my so-called enemies (it's all in the mind and how we perceive our challenges and so forth).

Truly, it is fascinating how our civilization has withstood so much harm. We are endowed with such a great reliance to forbearance. We are survivors of the best kind. We strive to do our best and achieve all our goals and dreams. When we don't, we may recognize that we are without. Being without, to me, exemplifies the notion that we are not listening to our intuition. We think that the mind chatter is at times being crazy and incompetent. When we can be quiet and relaxed into a tranquil environment and hook-up with our innate knowledge of being we connect with our soul. Our soul is pure and clean. It is the essential part of living and for a good living. Now, good living to me is not living in a mansion or in a castle, so to speak. Good living to me is being content and grateful for our existence and compelled to preserve and complete our highest potential and most importantly, to listen to our inner voice or our intuition. Do not become confused with the irrelevant and obsessive mind chatter. Do organize your thoughts and sieve through them and keep the good notions and intentions alive. Do good and you shall be rewarded.

At all times re-consider who you are grateful to and what you are grateful for. By regressing and looking at our past existence, as I mentioned earlier, acknowledge everything in your life, even the things that you thought brought you distress because those are, to me, the most important undertakings. Strive to renew yourself every day come rain or shine. Commend yourself and love yourself unconditionally as well as all your brothers and sisters as we are all part of a vast and limitless consciousness that is constantly evolving at a different pace and all of these are innately superb.

Awesome is the gratitude that I endure to this day. I am so very thankful for being alive and kicking. (I don't kick anyone, though, not even myself). I am in awe of our world and our Universe. I do hope that we may understand that as we know some things are not well here, we also know that we can learn to be content no matter the circumstance. Even if we see strife and vast victimization, and even if we ourselves have troubles and or heart-ache. It is the dire living that is a compelling truth of polarities that we need to try to understand, accept and endure.

In closing, I am eternally grateful for discovering and practicing Laughter Yoga. It is a well worth exercise and activity that encourages positive reinforcement in thoughts and thought processing. Practicing releases endorphins similar to a runners' high, as well as making us more child-like and hence freer. In being free, one can reach a plane of contentment and we join with other participants in camaraderie of sorts. The practice exists to perpetuate good feelings and it has a myriad of benefits just by retaining these. Together with meditation at its close, it intensifies gladness, acceptance and pure joy after exercising all our inner organs. It also alters the chemistry in the brain to rely in a more self-awaked state, clarity of mind and bliss.

Finally, be brave and don't ever give up because all is well and we are learning, reaching high altitudes, encompassing life strides sustaining an amicable smile to all.

NEGATIVE PERCEPTION

Alone in this world of mine

Very true but not at all so fine

To be here and Now

What is the answer, I ask?

How do we withhold the strain?

That is so hurtful in the plane

Hope for better days

Want to be held in strength

Please help me on my way

In reducing instinctly the haze

I do love this world of mine

And know I will rebound

When all is set and planned

In a timely frame of mind

UP UP AND AWAY

Appreciation is ascension to higher planes
With grace and love entwined in faith
Diverse rewards to encounter
And plenty sound of mind to revel
Reduce dispute and create
Divine solace today

CHAPTER 18

ACCEPTANCE

It is wonder when we are willing and declare ourselves that; we then ensure a beautiful path and greater living. It's not easy understanding the wonder that life is. Things get in the way and we forget to focus on important issues. Look at a baby and its limitless search for learning. Be like them. Learn their way. At this point in their lives they are just being and that too are what we need to retain, calmness of thought and a spotless spirit. Let's help ourselves to the lessening of turbulent thoughts, the peace of accepting the wonder that we are. We are beings of enlightened souls seeking rebirth and renewal. As a child we were always happy and contented we were surprised and had wonderful new experiences that brought us lightness and cheerfulness. Why not preserve this frame of mind and be unassuming, understanding, accepting of wondrous moments, wherever they may originate.

In essence not to absorb in negative information spoken, written or suggested to us by means of providing us useless instruction for living well. For example: When someone is troubled they may speak to us about some things that are concerning us but usually when they suggest a negative reaction, it is out of their own fear-based feeling. Because they are transmuting their own fears to us, they may inflict fear upon us which is easy to accept without noticing that it's not our fear. We may accept in our plight to resolve a challenge we may be facing. Wondering about our challenges is a good needed principle to have and is a good idea to hear others on their view of them, but when we hear others' solutions to our challenges we need to be very cautious at times so that we do not blindly agree what they are suggesting us to resolve to our perceived problem. It could well be that out of their own fear-felt reality they are coming through and translating it to you and suggesting a fearful and frightful outcome. Do listen fully, but recognize your own potential and clarify in your own mind with rationalization and get your own solution, usually it feels better to cognize your own ideas and solve the issue yourself in which way to empower yourself more and own your right choices. It's a good idea to seek counsel and guidance even if it's not implored as sometimes in our lives when we feel we need it, we can hear other's solutions but ultimately we are supposed to decide for ourselves when we have clarity in the mind and even after the counsel of friends or others it is great support system and we are grateful for having friends that care and want to assist us at times. Our gut never lies. Feel it and choose accordingly without fear. It is of great importance to acknowledge ourselves as our own master and as a master we own our predicaments and resolve our own issues or challenges in our own time and to our wondrous benefit because we own our decision for better or for worse and so does the learning goes. Approval from outside are for the most part unnecessary, this is left for your personality attentiveness which ego is desirous of.

With awareness, we can then determine how everyone's life experience is different being as we are unique individuals therefore this uniqueness is for sure ours to carry. Because our experience is unique, so are our feelings and our awareness of these as well. I believe and have learned that we need to experience all types of emotions so that we may know how different actions feel to us. Our world seems to believe that everything has to be fine and dandy but in reality, how would that help us in developing our minds, our new perceptions and so forth? In accepting and creating more awareness in ourselves the choice starts with us because everything is within us and without us.

If a mother pampers her child, doesn't let the child experience different normal emotions such as getting tired, becoming hungry or maybe not feeling sad and other types of feelings and is always on top of things with their children, they become used to inflexibility because they are used to the easy way. This may occur sometimes and we grow up to be dependent on having always to be satisfied whether it be with enough comforting food or having special comforts etc. I believe that we need to undertake some discomfort because if we don't, we set ourselves up for havoc and we become less flexible. When our minds become inflexible (notice I say "become" as we are not inflexible at the start) and have to have things done in a certain way. With this type of behavior comes control and we are in anticipation of the next thing we are going to do. For example; we have breakfast every day at 9 am but today for the reason that the plumber needs to come inside your house to make some repairs you didn't know this in advance, you are unable to keep your regular daily 9 am ritual. Now you are angry because it's impossible to keep your own appointment with your freak control of your time schedule. You may start blaming the bad timing for these repairs and you might even show a bad attitude to the repair person maintaining your own home plumbing and the HOA's procedures. This is one example I have made-up to explain our behaviors to do with inflexibility of the mind and we may attribute it to different things such as, control or loss of thereof, selfishness or always having things done our way or maybe we want to keep ourselves used to the repetition of frame of mind. In these cases, I believe that it is imperative that we are aware of our own conditioning and with this in mind we may be able to continually correct ourselves about the habits that we've created and those which might not serve us well. Even though a good habit of having breakfast every day at a certain time may be good for uniformity and health, it is also essential to break away at habits that keep us chained to inflexibility because it doesn't help us in the long run. As we get older there are two ways to the highway as I call it, the "Quick link" or the "Slow link" maybe go to the Interstate or take the road. Whichever you take you are choosing what you in your mind think is best for you. Now, if you are thinking solely of yourself as the whole population usually does, then is when we get into trouble as we are not supportive to others and who are there for us to accept, hopefully learn from and move on.

Remember what is known about "Everything happens for a reason?" The way I am aware of this suggestion is that if things happen, appointments get changed, accidents occur, love happens or not, dealings fail or succeed and the list goes on. We need to be aware that in order to become more resilient and attain more clarity we need to accept what is happening at all times. What good does it do us to be resentful of happenings? Why cry when the pail of water has tipped and we've lost its contents? Strike when the iron is hot and be accepting of what is and as a matter of fact, what is not! In the end, it is how we take things that keep us in a good state of health because no inner turmoil exists.

Remember that everything is within us and we can choose the right way. Knowing the right way may mean the proper action to be taken and used towards alleviating, consoling or fixing any situation which we either have created or we think that someone else has created for us, because we are ascribed with free will and do unto others what we would want done unto us; as the bible may quote. It makes sense doesn't it, to take the right responsibility in order to go on and be well.

When right is chosen instead of wrong there is an insatiable desire to do more of the same. The wheel is set in motion and we are aware and in control of it. We can defer and change but all is well when we change for our own goodness and well-being. We are innately good beings I can assure you that no-one wants to get up in the morning and think "I am going to do the worst I can do today"! We get up and we may be aware of concerns we need to deal with, jobs we need to get done and many things we want to accomplish. As none of us are perfect, we procrastinate, we pull cotton-wool over our eyes, we negate, we lie to ourselves, we don't do what we set out to do, etc. But when awareness becomes our middle name, we are in the present which we call it the gift. We know well what there's to be done and it's called "work." We need to work on ourselves because no-one is going to do this for us. We are on our own in the sense of the free will we so have and use daily indeterminately. Someone in my Toastmasters Club once gave a speech and he said "We do it to ourselves, yes". What he spoke about is that we have responsibility and it is essential to our good living to use it well and not give up things knowing that we need to complete them. We also create pain to our bodies when we overuse it, when we maybe don't consume enough food to keep healthy or even if we overeat and become sorely unhealthy. We could over-exercise, over-do is the word – do more than our bodies can maintain existing health or we hurt ourselves eating the wrong foods knowing well we have health issues and medical conditions where we need to adhere to a certain diet. The story is "We make ourselves hurt." Knowingly or in oblivion we do. Cease the endless pain, it seems like. Be more aware of the things you do daily, monthly, yearly or for evermore. See it, conquer it and mend it! Want something. Want to thrive in whatever your desire is, "Go for it." Go for it without stepping on rapid waters and without creating havoc in other people's lives. Become inner directed and you shall succeed in all your endeavors. Outer direction keeps a materialistic way of living where feelings are replaced by objects and possessions that may not serve us well at times. Beware of your thoughts as with anything else. I believe that if we change our thoughts we can automatically change our lives and we can do this to improve our existence as well as the people surrounding our circle ever presently. "Be well because "I am."

ACCEPTANCE

Benign is the love we give and take
Why not disperse of it more?
Cannot we keep well behaved?
Does this present a chore?
Task at hand may tempt us more
Give in to the torrent's shore
Share love, joy and peace
Receive, receive, receive

GENERATE PRESENCE

Open up to delight
Find hope, faith and lightness of heart
We have it in sight
Don't fool yourself any more
Do away with remorse
Arriving nowhere and won't get you anywhere
You decide where leads the road
With foresight it'll be the true passageway
Sincerity for yourself first
All will be well when the message is finally heard

SPELLBOUND

Enormous strides are made
Through our paths and our pacts
Toward wellness and resign
And toward fostering much love
For whom provide incline
To blessings and strings unattached
And with individual light
Intermittent light renewed
With akin lightness of heart endowed
This presents such blessings
Into the lives we have so diligently discovered
And implored with just decisions
As we become renewed, boundless and whole